HERE AND THERE

Poetry of Rural Prince Edward Island

By Roderick MacDonald

HERE AND THERE

Poetry of Rural Prince Edward Island

By Roderick MacDonald

The Acorn Press
Charlottetown
2020

ACORNPRESS

P.O. Box 22024
Charlottetown, Prince Edward Island
C1A 9J2
acornpresscanada.com

Edited by Hugh Macdonald
Illustrated and designed by Matt Reid
Printed in Canada

Title: Here and there / Roderick MacDonald.
Names: MacDonald, Roderick, 1960- author.
Description: Poems.
Identifiers: Canadiana 20200331361 | ISBN 9781773660653 (softcover)
Classification: LCC PS8625.D75225 H47 2020 | DDC C811/.6—dc23

The publisher acknowledges the support of the
Government of Canada, the Canada Council of the Arts
and The Province of Prince Edward Island.

For Gwen

Contents

1. The River

What awaits past the river bend?
What do we find today, my friend?
Water: pebbled by the western breeze
A blue jay shrieks in the poplar trees
The brook trout lies in the cool, dark deep
The eagle glides on her broad-winged sweep
A fisherman crouches on a rusty stool
A kingfisher's plunge, a concentric jewel
The child in the kayak has laughing eyes
Cirrus clouds paint the vaulted skies
Banks rise high with forest green
Black ducks dabble, bob, and preen
The paddles drip
The rushes sway
Last rays of sunlight
Fade away

Home awaits past the river bend
Guide the craft with me, my friend
As we float on the stream of sleep
The night wind stirs the leaves to quiver
Aspen trembles. Willows weep
While onward passes time, and river

2.   Alder Saplings

Birds sing here
In the alder saplings
Sprung from the field
We cut and abandoned
Mice run here
Through the grass tunnels
Hidden below
While the fox sniffs and waits
Trees sway here
When the West Wind travels
Tugs at the leaves
That rattle and tremble
Clouds float here
On a high blue canvas
Brush strokes above
Cast a cool shadow
Light shines here
Brother Sun Sister Moon
As Francis said
And the fireflies dance

3. In the Rain

With metronomic dripping
Eaves troughs are overflowing
Ditches all are filling
With September rain

And you run outside, dancing
With arms outstretched, and laughing
Your image seen distorting
Through the windowpane

Air smells of earth and ozone
Your hair is soaked and wind-blown
Your mouth catches a hail stone
As you drink the sky

Full, heavy raindrops tumble
Bold thunder starts to rumble
Your cold wet fingers fumble
Wet eyes make you cry

Mist rises from hot pavement
The gutter flows in torrent
Your eyes are wild and distant
Every surface gleams

Charcoal colour in the skies
And your dress clings to your thighs
I can almost hear your sighs
Now your damp face beams

Your dress now draped for drying
The rainstorm is subsiding
My world is redefining
Through the windowpane

Next time I won't stand looking
Instead I'll take you dancing
With arms around you laughing
In September rain

4.   Starlings

They gather, fierce and boisterous, loud and free
And clothe the leafless branch in proud display
The iridescent starlings in the tree

A race from far across the northern sea
They leave their new-found home in disarray
The gather, fierce and boisterous, loud and free

They bellow their discordant symphony
These brash newcomers from so far away
The iridescent starlings in the tree

Ruthless, they fulfill their destiny
And fling aside the ways of yesterday
They gather, fierce and boisterous, loud and free

They chatter loudly as they disagree
And cloak the New World colours all in grey
The iridescent starlings in the tree

Each one a fragment of a history
Each one must struggle, living day to day
They gather, fierce and boisterous, loud and free
The iridescent starlings in the tree

5. Morell River Bridge

East on the bridge to Midgell and Marie
Trucks cough and rattle along
West to Dunstaffnage or off to Dundee
Cars scoot across and are gone

Cyclists in file wobble west to Byrne's Road
East to Five Houses a tractor shakes past
Western bound campers with gear neatly stowed
Leather clad bikers cruise east and move fast

Highway above. River below
Like Jordan with tribes either side
Your deepest thoughts, Pilgrim; how can I know?
You move while I abide

Do you carry the luggage of hope or regret?
Do your passengers clash or agree?
Do you smile in remembrance or long to forget?
Whether west to Byrne's Road or east to Marie?

6. The Apple Tree

I paused beside the apple tree
The blossoms heaved with honeybees
Their heavy buzzing filled the air
And floated on the ocean breeze

June is here. Our time is now
The humming chorus seemed to say
Gather nectar. Harvest sweetness
Before the flowers fade away

The hour is now and time is short
From birth to death sweet summer's span
We dance as we were born to dance
And drink the nectar while we can

We dance as we were born to dance
Upon the air from tree to hive
No thought of past or future days
But scent and sound, awake, alive

7. Walk

Walk on through the sand and keep your own pace
Careful, the pebbles and shells can be rough
Smile as you go for this isn't a race

Speak gentle farewells and take leave with grace
Know that you sojourn is never enough
Walk on through the sand and keep your own pace

No-one to run from and no-one to chase
Sometimes refusing to play can be tough
Smile as you go for this isn't a race

Visit with others but find your true place
Don't heed the sales pitch it's all a big bluff
Walk on through the sand and keep your own pace

The grit in your eye and mud on your face
Is empty and fleeting, just ego stuff
Smile as you go for this isn't a race

Feet on the ground and eyes out to space
Stones that are thrown at you will scrape and scuff
Walk on through the sand and keep your own pace
Smile as you go for this isn't a race

8. The Christmas Card

The old card shows the marketplace
And snow adorns clock tower's face
This is the centre of our town
And Christmas brought us home

Rough benches in the Half Moon Inn
Many a pint, many a grin
That was the place we gathered then
When Christmas drew us home

We'd laugh and shoulder through the crowd
Fearless and happy, young and loud
Merv would pour us another round
As Christmas found us home

Then out into the winter street
Another bar, more folks to meet
And mistletoe and friendly girls
Now Christmas had us home

We fired our snowballs to the sky
At London House we said, *Goodbye*
Then, *Time* was called on Christmas Eve
At Christmas time at home

The walk back home was sweet and still
Past St. Marie's and down the hill
I'd eat chips under the stars
The Christmas stars of home

I'd fumble for the back-door key
And watch the moon shine through the tree
Then close the door on Christmas Eve
With Christmas thoughts at home

In the bleary dawn we unwrap gifts
Trudge off to mass through blowing drifts
Then eat and watch the Christmas shows
On Christmas Day at home

We'd pass the time on Christmas Day
Contented, not too much to say
For life flowed easily back then
Those Christmas times at home

But we were so much younger when
No longer boys but not quite men
The ties remained to bring us back
For Christmas time at home

Now when I see that marketplace
With snow upon clock tower's face
I know the ties that bind are loosed
This Christmas far from home

I look upon another view
And lay down memories anew
And hope our sons will feel the pull
Of Christmas here at home

9. Lawn Tractor

Brooding, I sit: your lawn tractor
Sit, biding my time in the shed
The lawns are covered with snow now
And summer lies some way ahead

Do I pine for sunny mornings?
Do I miss the scent of the rose?
No. I'm at peace in the darkness
Content with my winter repose

Hardly salubrious confines
Where plywood is splintered by ice
I feel my deck slowly rusting
And my wires are nibbled by mice

Summer rekindles my purpose
When you, human, pull out my choke
My engine will whir, then sputter
As I spew out clouds of blue smoke

Grass stalks will tremble before me
As I cut a swath through the field
Daisies are mere mower-fodder
Day lilies will whimper and yield

I'll tear the top from the ant nest
The cricket I'll chase from its lair
I'll stir the dust, the seeds, the dirt
And allergen cloud in the air

The clattering of my motor
As I bring the meadows to heel
Will frighten birds and small children
And my threadbare drive belt will squeal

In spring I'll roll out with vigour
In summer I'm boisterous and loud
The sun will gleam on my fenders
The beam from my headlight so proud

Meanwhile, I'll stay here; well hidden
Summer will arrive in due time
There's no rush to get mowing
A winter of leisure's no crime

Summer's the time when I flourish
It's just that I'm not ready now
Leave me unemployed with the rakes
Please don't fit me out with a plough

10. Ice Fishing

The sled scrapes the snow
Whipped by the wind
I plan to wait
Where the fish will be rising
Crystals in the air: silver
The temperature is falling

The tip of the auger falling
Into the ice scatters the snow
Shards splinter: silver
Metal rattles on ice. Wind
Catches the spray rising
Leaden arms force me to wait

Cold allows no time to wait
Bur erect the tent, as falling
Flakes swirl in the rising
Breeze. Pegs stick in the snow
And, ever present, the wind
Defies my shelter. Black in a world of silver

The jig gleams silver
I hunch and wait
Flicking the line while the wind
Drums the shelter. The jig is falling
Boots wear a patch in the snow
A shimmer of light: the first fish are rising

My pulse is rising
The spears flashes silver
A fish in the snow
I now wait
Eagerly. The spear poised, then falling
I, warm in the shelter, out of the wind

The rushing wind
Marks the fish count that's rising
The spear is still falling
A sharp flash of silver
No need to wait
Fish piled on the snow

Wind blowing the silver
Grains: dancing and rising. Wait
Until dusk in the light falling snow

11. February 14, 2017

The vixen shivers in her earthy den
A star shines high. An icy point of light
The farmer's field is frozen once again
Crystals dance in air on this winter night
The angry gusts now shake the frosty pane
Above the trees the hazy moon glows pale
I cast a glance around our room in vain
Alone, I sit and listen to the gale
Yet over empty miles our spirits touch
And warm us still, while icy Venus shines
Though far apart our love burns far too much
To be subdued by winter's cold confines
Tonight, we share the evening star
And realize no distance is too far

12. Flash Freeze

I am surprised. I thought I had more time
But streets glitter with icy menace
Free, easy movement a mere hour ago
Is now treacherous, after the flash freeze

Ice branches diffuse anaemic light
They rattle their tune to the north-west wind
Impossibly beautiful and fragile
Yet heavy; trees cower under such weight

Breath-sucking cold has flattened a car tyre
The wipers are frozen to the windshield
Amid a matrix of crystals serpents
While contrary doors deny their purpose

I am surprised. I thought we had more time
But your face is set; cold and resolute
Easy words spoken a mere hour ago
Now hang dead and still as a flash freeze

13. Christmas Tri-o-let

I hear the frozen river crack
And smell the smoke from wood stove fires
A sweet sound rings from Christmas choirs
I hear the frozen river crack
I hear the tale of wise men three
And decorate the Christmas tree
I hear the frozen river crack
And smell the smoke from wood stove fires

My footsteps scuff the dusting snow
I watch a star high up above
The season touches us with love
My footsteps scuff the dusting snow
I see the hungry blue jay feed
And gifts unwrapped with eager speed
My footsteps scuff the dusting snow
I watch a star high up above

Just now the houses dance with light
I see the TVs glow within
And soon the re-runs will begin
Just now the houses dance with light
And visions of our bygone days
Remembered through a mulled wine haze
Just now the houses dance with light
I see the TVs glow within

The evening air is breathless calm
I feel the peace that Christmas brings
When children dance and Crosby sings
The evening air is breathless calm
The season weaves a magic spell
Enchanted by the Christmas bell
The evening air is breathless calm
I feel the peace that Christmas brings

14. Redde Mudde

Stuck in a boggy April lane
Called for help to tow me free
The driver leaned against his winch
And spoke these words to me

Two hundred million years ago
A mighty lake once lay
Triassic critters splashed about
Where now runs this byway

Salt beds and sandy sediment
Into bedrock were pressed
Foundations laid for PEI
The island we love best

The Ice Age scraped and carved this land
With sheets near two miles thick
Red earth was ground and pushed around
That now lies wet and slick

The glaciers retreated then
And water levels rose
Our Island fair, well-watered mud
Wherein you now repose

No common, ordinary dirt
But real primeval muck
Laurasian sand with provenance
Now THAT'S what got you stuck

15. North Shore

Watch the horizon reach to the sky
Feel the strong, relentless tides
Smell the seaweed and brine on the air
Hear the gull's cry as she glides

Dip your feet in the edge of the deep
Wade in the ocean of time
Splash your face with the tears Jesus wept
Let the sea cleanse the sin and the grime

Hark to the ripples sibilant rush
As they flood the drowning sand
And draw comfort, you, son the Earth
For the sea-mother cradles her land

The spirit still moves on the water
And the trackless oceans know
That, while we ride on the full spring tide
Fortunes ebb just as well as they flow

16. Presence

He walks the beach where moonlight shines clear
Hears the hesitant harbour bell
Smells the salt where the sea laps the pier
While the harbour light stands sentinel
And he stares at the deep ocean's swell

My father's spirit fills this windswept bay
My father's wisdom is voiced by the sea
Out here a man can breathe and pray
Sand and spray set his bound soul free
And it's here Father's hand touches me

17. Rossiter Park, November

A goldfinch flits from bough to bough
(Flowers flamed. Now rosehips wane.)
His once bright coat is faded now
Summer sun left autumn rain

We sat there then and watched the stream
Silently, we watched the tides
Cars on the bridge flowed east and west
Nought we cherished now abides

I sit now in the north wind's chill
Trees wear yellow rags of time
The mottled finch is singing still
Hissing reeds attend his thyme

Dead leaves: float, eddy, dart, and turn
Pontoon docks are hauled ashore
Our haunted souls recall and yearn
Hoping for our spring once more

18. The Nest

I saw your nest while working
Frail on an aspen tree
Enduring yet abandoned
A woven filigree

The grass that you had gathered
And placed in flowing rills
Has stood the test of winter storms
A credit to your skills

You're driven by instinct and passion
I build with tools and plans
Your thoughts are of the present
So different from Man's

We know inexorable time
Will cause our work's decay
We know nothing lasts forever
I'm fool to hope it may

You will build again this springtime
As you are wont to do
And I wonder fellow builder
Who's craftsman me or you?

19. Wisdom of the Wood

If we ask, the trees will know
And share the wisdom of the wood
If we ask
How to stand the axe's blow
How roots dig deep and branches grow
How to live just as we should
If we ask

If we look, we might see
Questions answered in the glade
If we look
Why saplings must grow free
Why knowledge hangs upon a tree
Why we need the sacred shade
If we look

If we listen, we may hear
Whispered comfort in the leaves
If we listen
Where dew hangs like a dropping tear
Where the singing wind is ever near
Where plays the tune that nature weaves
If we listen

20. Sunday Morning

Sunlight is our dawn alarm
Another slice of toast with tea?
Waking faces worn 'til noon
'Phone in shows on CBC
Feel the joy the weekend brings
All is just as it should be
Home on Sunday morning

Children laughing in the park
Climbing high on the pirate ship
Up the ladder, down the slide
Giving Mom and Dad the slip
Daddy push me on the swing
All is just as it should be
Home on Sunday morning

(Friendly faces wait in pews)
Stride churchward in your Sunday best
(Sunday saints, and the sincere)
Calm and smiling, neatly dressed
Listen to the choir sing
All is just as it should be
Home on Sunday morning

Hear the boater chug upstream
Churns the rushes in his wake
Runs an oversized outboard
Speeding hard for speeding's sake
Ripples in a sparkling ring
All is just as it should be
Home on Sunday morning

Blessed are the merciful
Blessed also the pure in heart
Blessed are the peaceful ones
On Sunday we all play our part
Holy angel, soar on wing
All is just as it should be
Home on Sunday morning

21. The Cottage

I'm thinking

Of
Propane grilling
Beer can fizzing
Patio lights

Of
Dewy mornings
Firefly evenings
Starry nights

Where
The nesting goshawk shrieks
The mad-cap squirrel cheeps
And love-sick peepers fill the vernal choir

Then
Times when all is silent
Beneath the Milky Way
As embers pop and dance around the fire

I'm wishing

That
June, July, and August
A shining span of time
Could compass our existence
And make our year sublime

22. Crow

Wings beat beat beat
Methodically
Fly to your roost
Generations
Have passed this way
Where hemlocks grew
Now buildings stand
Still you fly here
Inky black eyes
Seek carrion
Or tired song birds
To feed your brood

Wings hiss hiss hiss
Hypnotically
In the dusk air
Unstoppable
Impulse on high
Seeking using
And adapting
While you call out
Cold metallic
Not a sweet song
But a hoarse cry
In the vastness

Wings flap flap flap
Bewitchingly
Against the sky
Intelligence
Of the ages
Race memories
Of maple groves
And salmon runs
Into the now
Always striving
For your crow kind
Most human bird

23. Georgie the Cat

How can I write
When this evil sprite of
A cat
The brat
Does rounds?

It leaps and runs
Instruction it shuns. This
Grey brat
The cat
Confounds

Did Tolstoy
Own a Donskoy?
Nyet, boy!

Did E A Poe
Have a calico?
I don't think so

Chasing, jumping, pouncing
Stealthily....
Creeping....
Then
Racing, tumbling, spinning

Then the wretch
Will....
Lazily....
Stretch
And purr

In sun she'll soak
And I will stroke
Her fur

24. Incantation

Breath of air. A summer breeze
Scent of blossom in the trees

Smile of stranger. Laugh of child
Whitecaps on the ocean wild

Hand of friendship. Touch of care
Worn and favoured easy chair

Crystal mornings. Sunny dawn
Dew drops shining on the lawn

Gentle kisses. Lover's smile
Sandy beaches of the isle

Busy kitchens. Voices loud
Peaceful walks far from the crowd

Evening rain. Thunder roll
July mare with newborn foal

Blessings dance beneath the skies
Light the fire behind your eyes

25. Bill

By the river every morning
Sitting on the mossy bank
Bill fished motionless and quiet
Breathing air musty and dank

On the laneway every noon-time
Trudging homeward without care
With fishing rod and empty bucket
Jacket stained and thin with wear

Villagers would call out to him
Hey, Bill, what you catch today?
He just smiled and replied slowly
Every last one got away

Yet he sat there every morning
Grey eyes fixed as if entranced
While his line lay in the water
Nature all around him danced

Brook trout flashed in dappled shadows
Poplar branches cracked the sky
Squirrels scampered through the bushes
Eagles looked down from on high

Bright marigolds shining yellow
Matched the goldfinch with their show
While across the woods and marshes
Rang the hoarse cry of the crow

Skeins of geese with raucous honking
Silent, deadly osprey dive
Bullfrogs with their basso chatter
Brought the swampy fields alive

'Though he knew no wife nor children
'Though he called no man his friend
Bill felt all creation near him
Peace upon him did descend

By the river one spring morning
Dead beside the mossy brook
When then reeled his line in for him
They found that it bore no hook

26. Carol

I knew you barely; to my detriment
You strode through the village quite self-possessed
You graced my rough verse with kind interest

People spoke of your humble temperament
I heard the tales of those who knew you best
I knew you barely, to my detriment
Your strode through the village quite self-possessed

Gone away and I sometimes still lament
Let me make my affection manifest
To me you gave, unknowing, a bequest
You graced my rough verse with kind interest
Your strode through the village quite self-possessed
I knew you barely, to my betterment

27. Island Breeze

The West Wind
Leaps from the Gulf
Plays in the waves
Sings in the surf
Rattles the sand
Island breeze
Tousles your hair
Tugs at your dress
Calms at sunset
Sleeps with the night

28. Wild Roses

The scent of a single wild rose
Lost in the wind
Apart; obscured by the leaves
Pale in the sun
Anonymous
Hidden

Then
In sweeping beds beside the trail
Shine twilight pink
Delicate primeval perfume
Pervades the air
A fragrant bank of wild roses

29. Local Daily, A1: Truck Collides with Horse and Buggy*

Immortal Xanthus; child of the West Wind
The Furies accost you
Brave Achilles struggles to hold your rein

Winged Pegasus; sprung from evil blood
Slip your golden bridle
Let arrogance plunge from high Olympus

Old nag with buggy and Amish farmer
Rear-ended by a truck
Let the fool, next time, clean off his windshield

*Inspired by *The Guardian,* Prince Edward Island

30. Hope Returns

Hope returns like a robin in spring
Cheerily sings out *Cheerio*
Gaudy brick red coat on show
Bold in thawing snow

Hope returns like a wave on the sea
Broken free from the winter freeze
Rolling by the fishing quays
Chasing with the breeze

Hope returns like the sun's rising light
Lifting from the grey horizon
Warming all it rests upon
Bidding doubt *Begone*

Hope returns like an old promise
A lock that has found a key
An answer to a plea
From deep within me

31. Girl with a Kite

The girl with the kite
Is captured by the south wind
She surrenders

She fears the gust's strength
Her father calls instructions
She doesn't hear

She thrills at the tug
A 'phone records
The girl is unaware

She clings to the line
Salt rushes to her nostrils
She doesn't sense it

She resists the weight
Hot sun kneads her neck

She feels nothing
But the dread of flying
And the urge to fly

Released

She leaves
And looks back at the sand in the wind

32. Blueberry Jam

On a hidden shelf
In a jar of heavy glass
Deep dark and thick
Preserved while time has passed

In the dusty basement
With heirloom threadbare tablecloths
Discarded Tupperware
Where cedar guards against the moths

Bottled joy of that August day
Along the edge of the berry field
You trod lightly as you gleaned
I awkward as I kneeled

Under the sun
Quiet but for bee buzzing and bird song
That filled the arching sky
All afternoon long

33. St. Peter's Harbour Lighthouse

Frail timber bones do rot with salty spray
A clinging darkness falls where once shone light
Does aged skin of shingle fade to grey?
Time's arrows sting and wind-blown sand grains bite
The Harbour is an echo of the past
Boats now content at Red Head Wharf to tie
No schooner's lookout climbs a lofty mast
Consigned, your tower seems, to rot and die
But Pharos' beacon never did resound
With laughing sounds so joyful and alive
Folks seeking sun and solace now abound
As down the rutted lane the people drive
St Peter's Harbour Light endure and stand
Where mermaids lie on beach towels on the sand

34. Wedding Wish

As you walk amid the mountains
Beside the deep, cool lake
And you feel the rush of living
With each new step you take
Then you wonder what adventures
The coming years will bring
May all your troubles melt away
Like snow drifts in the spring

Then when you visit PEI
As we all think you must
You'll head out to the Lighthouse Beach
Down roads of red clay dust
You'll remember where you came from
While walking on the sand
And dreams will seem so limitless
When dreaming hand in hand

35. Know Your Limit

Life is frenetic and busy
You drive like a bat out of Hell
But the posted limit is *Fifty*
So slow down as you drive through Morell

Aubrey pulls out of the restaurant
Still thinking about what he ate
If you're whipping by doing eighty
He may have T-bone on his plate

Old George leaves the funeral home
He radiates quietude
Don't drive too fast and smash-up the hearse
Better to be seen than viewed

You really can't miss the school zone
The sign is not hard to discern
Speeding in here will double your fine
That's a hard lesson to learn

The road descends past the Irving
That's no place to drive like an ass
Besides , that's my road; the turn is tight
Please keep your foot off the gas

You can speed up past the river
As you bid our village, *Farewell*
You can steer back into the fast lane
But slow down as you pass through Morell!

*penned to remind both visiting and local drivers!

36. Considered Opinion

I think; I should like to have a drink
And contemplate your question for a while
Perhaps consider all the pros and cons
We'll resolve this little impasse with a smile

Breathe deeply and remember how to smile
A sensible decision with no cons
Will be afforded in a little while
But first, I think; I should have a drink

I think; I will have a pint of beer
And cogitate upon the facts in hand
Sagacity and tact inform our choice
Take time to ruminate before we stand

Now, seeing as I know just where you stand
I hope you see the wisdom of my choice
And, surely, you will offer me you hand
That is, when I have drunk this pint of beer

A velvet curtain draws across my eyes
My head is heavy and my spirit light
Are we sorted out? Did we come to terms?
My will to think has fallen with the night

I trust time passed enjoyably this night
I feel we understood each other's terms
Soon will come the dawning of the light
And now I'm going to close my weary eyes

37. About a Mile

About a mile from here to there
Twenty minutes or thereabout
A pilgrimage to seek the shore
A holy walk for the devout

From heathen pavement to the lane
Where twisted apple trees grow wild
The farmhouse yard is worn and bare
A firewood altar neatly piled

On either side fields roll away
Behind the weathered tractor shed
A spirit wind blows from the Gulf
And pious barley bows its head

A narrow track now leads the way
The birches form a leafy vault
Their branches intertwine above
And with their art our God exalt

The shaded lane sweeps down and left
Where puddles fill with summer rain
A font where starlings splash about
And make baptismal vows again

Birds in the bushes left and right
Scatter and soar up to the sky
Angelic feathers fluttering
Carrying praise to Her on high

The path now broadens flanked by pools
A great blue heron tall and straight
Decides which fish will pass or not
Just like Saint Peter at the gate

The final climb between the dunes
Reveals a beach of Island sand
A prayer of thanks escapes my lips
For I have reached the Promised Land

38. Gravity

I forget the sound of you voice
Memories of you are dying

The dunes are invisible now
Under this waning moonlight
A patch of ocean shines, then fades
A hint of something indistinct
Forms surrender to the night
Ghosts of past and future partings?

Perhaps I hear the bell-buoy ring
Or pebbles tumble; I'm unsure

Now forgiving amnesia
Blesses me with its blurred edges

Our bond is weakened with distance
Like gravity that moves the tides

39. Landing Day

On the wharf; red-eyed in the dawn
Uncles, aunts, and cousins
Trucks in the lot. Work gloves at hand
Beer on ice in dozens

The first load is in around six
Everyone's fit and spry
Weighted and soaked, traps hit the dock
You want them stacked HOW high?

The captain, then, sails out again
Past the end of the pier
Hopefully, he'll be gone an hour
Someone opens a beer

The *Alpine* and *Schooner* are flowing
Banter starts - friend to friend
Can't work with that shit on your gloves
Not there, the other end!

Some captains are quiet and patient souls
Alas, but some are not
Most work the day quite cool and calm
Some yell and curse a lot

The old guys lean against the traps
And give their five cents worth
Wouldn't cross the harbour with him
Not safe to leave the berth

The traps pile higher and higher
Rope coiled like bleached-out snakes
The dock help is more subdued now
Each landing brings fresh aches

Now all have brought the last load in
But one boat is mistook
They left a trawl in the ocean
Cork saw but didn't look

The helpers take home their lobster
Glad to be on their way
Happy to lift, and push, and pull
But only for one day

Nothing remains by wind-blown cans
Traps dry in the June sun
Peace and calm; rum for the skipper
Another season done

40. Murder

Today I witnessed a murder
And to my dismay
Frozen in sick fascination
I could not look away

I tried to move and turn
From what my eyes beheld
But I was rooted to the spot
Enthralled and yet repelled

I could perhaps have stopped
This gruesome shadow play
That ran its course in silence
While I spied across the way

The victim was quite helpless
Eyes terrified and wild
Attacked, abused, and broken
A toy with an angry child

The killer struck with venom
Paused then struck again
Playing with the victim
Showing arrogant disdain

I stayed concealed and quiet
And watched the violent spree
Alive with guilty interest
Like watching reality TV

Thank God the horror ended
And I crept from my coward's hide
The cat slunk off to a sunny spot
The mouse, alas, had died

41. Sanctum Sanctorum

Your beach wrap flutters in the air
Its hem it tinged with salty spray
The sun has met us here again
All the way from yesterday

Your sunscreen leaves a soft, deep sheen
It glistens like so many jewels
While wavelets whisper to the shore
And scatter through the sandy pools

You kick your shoes into the sand
Then stretch your legs out from your chair
Grains flow and tumble through your toes
You sit back; happy, unaware

You're bathed in sunlight, lulled by waves
Your mind is calm. You're out of reach
I'd be a fool to break this spell
Disturb the sanctum of the beach

Now evening breezes stir the grass
The summer sun will soon sink low
Our mood will shift just like the sand
And we will pack our things and go

But then I will remember where
Your beach wrap fluttered in the air

42. Summer 2018

Do not complain of summer's scorching heat
While blazing sunlight burns a clear blue sky
'Though dry dust whirls and scatters in the street
And farm crops wither in its golden eye
When every little movement makes you sweat
Your fan spins fast and circuits overload
Come evening by mosquitoes you're beset
And tourist traffic slows you on the road
But: off to the beach, and river, wood, and trail
Sunscreen and bug repellent help your cause
Too soon the July sunlight starts to fail
And then your mind will dwell on winter's flaws
So, friend, lest summer's lustre starts to fade
Go pour yourself a drink and find some shade

43. Acadian Bell

Hear the bell
The Acadian bell
Soft as the enduring murmur of the sea
Hear the souls whisper

Hear the bell
Muffled in the red earth
Buried in an unmarked grave; long forgotten
Rusting with the bones

Hear the bell
Gentle like the soft wind
Between the gnarled birches marking the abandoned farm
Sentries guarding orchards' bitter fruit

Hear the bell
Echoing through time
Tolling for lost and banished generations
Bequeathing the horizon and the names

White, Pitts, Perry, and King
Still the bells of Acadie ring
Ancient names re-forged and true
Acadian bells cast anew

44. Cycling on the Beach

I'm cycling on the beach
Out of reach
Alone
No 'phone
Unplanned
On the sand
Breathing air
Without care

Tyres hiss
Nothing amiss
Where I find bliss

Barely a sound but the sea whispering
Merely a thought that I'm following

Cloudlets above
Tracks beneath

Nothing to know
Nothing worth knowing
Nowhere to go
That's where I'm going

Pedals spin
I grin

Diamond sea
And me
We're free

45. Ebb Tide

The ebb tide reveals
Smooth, naked sand
Pebbly shallows
The breakwater's skeleton

The moon hunts the clouds
To the horizon
And casts a golden path
To the edge of the world

46. Rip Tide

Here in the rip tide
In heaving swells of jade
Away I glide

I fought, I tried
Breathless and dismayed
Here in the rip tide

Away from my family's side
Figures on the shore now fade
Away I glide

Lost upon the ocean wide
By the rolling sea betrayed
Here in the rip tide

On summer streams I once did ride
Here's the price that must be paid
Away I glide

With ghosts I abide
Today I died
Here in the rip tide
Away I glide

47. Where the Girl Rests

At the river's edge
A pine tree dies
Its roots cling to the bank

Birds nest there
And squirrels run
Ripple-dancing sunlight
Paints its leaves

Mosses carpet its shade
Where the girl rests
And gazes at
The reed beds

At the river's edge
A pine tree lives
Its roots caress the bank

48. Under this Moon

Each wave returns to the sea

Brazen cresting crashing breakers
Announce themselves with a roar
Bite at the land and rip
With gravel claws

Constant heaving swelling rollers
In sensible order
With rhythmic slap and fizzing retreat
Leave their track

Gentle scurrying spreading ripples
Apologize to the sand
Form timid eddies around the pebbles
And melt away

Yet
Each wave returns to the sea
Ever gone
Ever present
In the bay
Under this moon

49. Here and There

Far past these security gates
A winding red clay road awaits
Uncompromising rows of guards
Make way for lupins lining yards
From vinyl chairs, plate glass, and heat
To bird song on the front porch seat
No more departures gone awry
But tell me when the tide is high
Now concrete runways lined with 'planes
Soon honking geese aloft in skeins
Farewell to baggage carousels
I'll greet the rolling North Shore swells

50. This Evening

Now we are tired
let's drink red wine
and reflect
and look to the West for a while

Then sleep
and dream of
the sun's heat
the waves rush
and the faces

Tomorrow
we will half remember
and invent absent memories

As we do

Until, again, we are drawn to the shore